CW00925727

SIGNIFICANT OTHER

Martin Scott

Explorations in Theology

- volume two -

Boz Publications Ltd.
71-75 Shelton Street - Covent Garden - London - WC2H 9JQ - United Kingdom.
office@bozpublications.com / www.bozpublications.com

Copyright © 2020 Martin Scott
First published 2020 by Boz Publications Ltd

The right of Martin Scott to be identified as the author of this work has been asserted by them in accordance with the Copyright, Designs and Patents Act 1988.

All rights reserved. No part of this publication may be reproduced, stored in a retrieval system, or transmitted in any other form or by any means, electronic, mechanical, photocopying, recording or otherwise, without the prior written permission of the authors. Permissions may be obtained by writing to the author at: martin@3generations.eu

ISBN: 978-1-9164216-4-6

A CIP catalogue record for this book is available from the British Library.

Contents

The Man named the cattle, named the birds of the air,
named the wild animals; but he didn't find a
suitable companion. God put the Man into a
deep sleep. As he slept, he removed one of his ribs
and replaced it with flesh. God then used the rib
that he had taken from the Man to make Woman
and presented her to the Man. The Man said,
"Finally! Bone of my bone, flesh of my flesh!
Name her Woman for she was made from Man".

– *(Genesis 2: 21-23)* –

When they got to Jesus, they saw that he
was already dead, so they didn't break his legs.
One of the soldiers stabbed him in the side
with his spear. Blood and water gushed out.

– *(John 19: 33-34)* –

A SUITABLE CO-WORKER

PREFACE

I KNOW THOSE WORDS

There are problematic words that we encounter whenever we talk theology or read Scripture. 'God' is certainly one of those, because the word has to be filled with some measure of understanding. In the first volume, I wrote on the 'wrath' of God, and if we were to dip into how God is viewed, I suspect for many 'anger' would be in there somewhere. Thankfully Jesus came as the express image of the deity that can only ultimately be known through encountering the Person of Jesus. God is the 'Jesus-like' God. So much so that Jesus said that only through him could one come to the 'Father'. The promise was not that through Jesus we would come to god (or God) but to come into a knowledge of who this 'God' was. That is not a one-off experience but something that is ongoing.

In the world of inter-faith, the question Christians often ask is, 'But is Allah God?'. The honest response I think is 'it depends'. It depends in the same way as we could ask the question, 'Is the 'Christian god God?' It depends!

If a Christian were to say, 'God punished my family by taking away our baby child,' I think the vast majority of us would push back (gently) that God does not do that. At that point, the 'god' being described is not 'God'. Probably in truth we all have a 'god' who is less than the God that Jesus revealed. Given the relational nature of the Christian faith, we are gladly in the process of getting to know the God and Father of our Lord Jesus Christ. It is a process, and we have to continue to update our understanding.

Updating our understanding is a constant provocation as we sometimes have to jettison something that we held on to prior to the update. Updating becomes more difficult when we encounter a word or a concept that we are sure we have got right, so much so that every time we come to read the word in the Scriptures we repeatedly give it the meaning we have always given it. Maybe one of the most difficult words to re-read is the word 'church'. It is also very difficult to re-read because theologically little work has been done on it as most theologians are usually intrinsically related to the concept behind the word they are seeking to theologise about.[1] As I write the pages that follow, I will often use the term 'body of Christ' or 'Christian community' when I refer to what others might term 'church'. I will do this as a small contribution to help us from defaulting to what we know, as well as for a theological reason that I will expand on later. At the end of the last volume, I wrote of the pierced side of Jesus indicating symbolically that out of his side might come forth an equal partner to fulfil the mandate of the original commission given to Adam and Eve.[2]

There are three broad approaches to church. There is the

1: 'Ecclesiology has often been one of theology's least innovative and interesting loci. Systematic theology has often served well-established institutions, and rigidified and legitimized their doctrines and practices. Rather than inquiring afresh into the church's nature and its mission in the world, theologians have sometimes been more anxious to defend those structures which paid their salaries.' (Finger, *Christian Theology*, Vol. 2 (Scottdale: Herald, 1989), p. 225f. Finger's comments are not to be limited to theologians, and the term 'salary' could be extended to include position, authority, esteem honour etc.

2: Although I do not believe in a literal Adam and Eve I am happy to use the language, the stories are rich and the concept and contrast of Adamic humanity and New humanity is certainly a biblical theme. That concept can be held on to without necessarily resorting to a crude belief in 'original sin'. In Mark 16:15, the commission of preaching was to proclaim the message to all of 'creation'. Something beyond simply 'all people' seems to be in view and the resonance with the commission to the primal humans seems clear.

institutional, appealing to the traditional approach, with an emphasis on the sacraments. The concept roughly runs along the following lines. Jesus instituted the church, Peter being key within that. Flowing on from Scripture, tradition helps us see that there is a form that developed with ordained clergy representing deity to us and serving as mediators of the divine life. In the extreme, it might have a very rigid class of (male) priests and provided one participates in the appointed sacraments one is 'saved'. That approach can have less rigid shapes, but ultimately the ongoing life of the believer is enhanced by partaking of the mass/eucharist with that part of the service normally being the focal point.

In the pre-Reformation era that was all-but the only form of church, the hope of salvation was tied up with belonging to this authoritarian institution. The Reformation reacted to this and emphasised belief (faith) as the means to salvation. It was not now an issue of belonging to the right institution but of being justified by faith. Hence there was a shift from 'priesthood' to 'ministers of the word'. The altar as the central focus gave way to the pulpit; the mass to the sermon. Those to be ordained were to be theologically astute. Belonging to the institution was replaced by faith, and growth would now take place through listening to the sermon so that right beliefs might develop.

There are of course, overlaps in the above two approaches, but the Reformation brought a clear divide to them. There is the suggestion that there is a third approach, and those who write struggle for the right term to describe this. Lesslie Newbiggin, in his book The *Household of God* simply used the term 'Pentecostal' for the third approach.[3] This term, though, is probably inadequate as many Pentecostal/charismatic groups are firmly within the 'pulpit/sermon/ belief' approach. Newbiggin's point though remains. Church can be centrally shaped and defined in a number of ways. It can appeal to institutional authority, or a claim to have the authority of Scripture,

3: London, SCM, 1953 / New York: Friendship, 1954.

or to be more loosely defined by the presence and activity of the Holy Spirit. It seems from history that many times there are ad hoc groups that begin life in this semi-anarchic (third-)way but are before too long domesticated! In using the term, semi-anarchic I could be flagging up an inherent danger or that 'anarchy' is often defined from a status quo perspective. We might wish to ask if Jesus was semi-(or totally-)anarchic and whether the Pauline communities were also.

I would also suggest that our perspectives (and so reading of Scripture) reflect our own personal preferences and perhaps also a reflection of our personalities. Strong leadership that is ever-so-certain in the midst of a shifting world, particularly if they also have a strong apocalyptic approach of impending doom, will gather around them those who by nature have anxiety issues. The strength of leadership helps soothe the anxieties! I do not write this to be cynical but to acknowledge that none of us are 'free', coming to situations and the Scriptures. We all have our distinct biases that come from the traditions that have impacted us and our own internal flaws.

We are 2000 years removed from the world of the New Testament; the 'faith world' has seen so many changes since then, and likewise, the political world has shifted enormously, so it is very difficult to know, for example, what was deep in Paul's mind when he was planting 'church' in city after city across the Empire. If we come to the narrative with a pre-set idea (as I have done), then we are likely to assume Paul was planting something just like I attended week by week. We have our answer, and it is very difficult to come to another conclusion or even to ask a question that might suggest another answer. Our presupposition simply provides our answer. What if, in the same way that we can be guilty of making 'God' in our image, we have been guilty of making 'church' in an image of something that we have already conceptually created.[4]

4: I appreciate that there are those who wish to add 'tradition' to the discussion, and therefore how 'church' and theology has developed over the past 2000 years also becomes an important element. It does not take too long to read between the lines I write that I am not of that school. Hence these volumes are a contribution, a perspective.

Is Jesus God?

The question is one of those 'orthodox' test questions. If we answer with the affirmative we are orthodox, for the creeds, tradition and the Scriptures all push us to say, yes he was God. However, one flaw! 'Is Jesus God' presupposes we know who (what) God is. If I know who God is, then I can decide if Jesus is God. The flaw in the statement was exposed by Jesus himself. He made it clear that if we have seen Jesus, then we have seen the Father (God). We might be able to know something about God outside of the personal revelation that comes through Jesus, as there is some measure of revelation in creation, and through that revelation we can be impacted by God's power and otherness to us, but to know who this God is we would have to go beyond that level of revelation. The question, 'Is Jesus God', can be asked but it also has to be quickly shelved. We really are inadequate to define Jesus in 'God-terms', but thankfully we can describe God in 'Jesus terms'. If we insist on the 'Is Jesus God?' question being answered, we could produce a distorted image of Jesus and sadly in distorting the image of Jesus we would never be able to know who God is.

Likewise, we can make a theologically 'correct' statement that probably also needs to be shelved. That statement is 'the church is the body of Christ'. True, but what if we have a distorted view of 'church', and the danger is we will continually start with the presupposition that we know what 'church' is, making it very difficult to break out of the circle.

The Jewish leaders understood that Jesus' activity, behaviour and teaching suggested that there was in measure an intrinsic claim of divinity. His behaviour pointed somewhere. In contrast to this, Jesus made a counterclaim against the same Jewish leaders. He did not acknowledge them as descendants of Abraham because of their murderous intent; he saw them as sons of 'their father' the devil! In both cases, the behaviour and activity suggested a conclusion.

It is the behaviour of the people who claim to follow Jesus that I consider can legitimise their claim (or otherwise) to be the church. In other words, it would be better to turn the above statement around and to suggest that 'the body of Christ is the church'. We know what 'church' is, but do we know what 'the body of Christ' is? And if we do not know what the body of Christ is, do we really know what church is? The body of Christ is seen through her actions and behaviour. For this reason, I will tend to use the term 'body of Christ' in these pages. It is vital that we rediscover what it means to be the body of Christ; otherwise, we could well settle for something less than that and label it 'church'.[5]

Healthy groups

Many institutions carry an internal sickness where they do not help release the destiny of those who belong, but rather they take the life from the people. A 'church' group can also fall into this trap, and the longer a history any institution has, the more liable it is to develop a set culture. In Scripture, this is termed 'Babylonish', where the survival of the institution is the goal that everyone has to serve.

In contrast, there are two ways in which a healthy group can be seen. They can be described as a **community** where the primary reason for being together is 'for one another'. By participating in the life of that group, I am encouraged and strengthened, thus becoming a better version of myself. The transformation of the members of the group then becomes very important.[6] The other way a healthy

---

5: This is not a criticism of what terms itself 'church', neither is it in pursuit of some ideal, as in the 'correct way to do church'. It is intended rather to allow for an exploration of diverse possibilities and to promote freedom that releases the body of Christ from the prison of conformity to preconceived ideas and forms. I fully acknowledge the fallenness of anything this side of the parousia even that which is shaped by Scripture. They are shaped by our reading of Scripture, and they are shaped by the likes of you and me!

6: Paul's letters are full of exhortations concerning how we relate to 'one another', based in his belief that we are 'individually members of one another' (Rom. 12:5), hence we should 'prefer one another', 'serve one another', 'forgive one another', 'not lie to one another'. The list goes on.

group can be described is as a **movement** where the primary reason for being together is not for the sake of one another but to bring about change in the world beyond the group. A good example of the latter could be the civil rights movement. Holding to a vision of a different world,[7] they set themselves through their plans and activity to change the world view of the wider world in which they sit, so that eventually a transformation would take place there. The mission is the reason for their existence; that mission being focused on a change in the wider world, with a healthier world appearing. If that health were to come then the reason for the existence of such a movement would become obsolete.

In presenting the two elements above, I have presented them as opposites, as an either/or choice. In reality, they do not need to present us with a binary choice, and when we come to the pages of the New Testament, we can see both elements as applicable to the body of Christ. As noted, there are numerous 'one another' exhortations embedded within Paul's letters that he wrote to localised Christian communities, and perhaps that aspect is the easier one to focus on, but I think to do so is to miss the essential missional nature of the partner who came forth from Jesus' side.

7: Timelessly captured in Martin Luther King's speech, 'I have a dream'.

CHAPTER 1

THE UNFINISHED WORK

On the cross, there is the cry that went up from the lips of Jesus that 'it is finished' and we are forever grateful for the truth that speaks of. We cannot add to the work of Christ... or can we?

In the light of the shout from the cross and also some of the clear Pauline teaching, there is a provocative Scripture to come to terms with in Colossians 1: 24-29. I quote below with emphasis added:

> *Now I rejoice in what I am suffering for you,*
> *and I fill up in my flesh* **what is still**
> **lacking in regard to Christ's afflictions,**
> *for the sake of his body, which is the church.*
> *I have become its servant by the commission*
> *God gave men to present to you the word*
> *of God in its fullness - the mystery that has*
> *been kept hidden for ages and generations,*
> *but is now disclosed to the Lord's people.*
> *To them God has chosen to make known among*
> *the Gentiles the glorious riches of this mystery,*
> *which is Christ in you, the hope of glory.*

He is the one we proclaim,
admonishing and teaching everyone
with all wisdom, so that we may present
everyone fully mature in Christ.
To this end I strenuously contend with all
the energy Christ so powerfully works in me.

He writes about filling up what 'is still lacking in regard to Christ's afflictions'.[1] A bold statement but one I consider does not contrast the understanding that Jesus fulfilled the mission the Father gave him to do. Hence the cry that **'It'** was finished, but the mission of the body, the appropriate partner has not been finished. This theme of the Father's mission to the Son and the Son's mission to the disciples seems very clear.

As you sent me into the world,
I have sent them into the world.

– *(John 17:18)* –

Again Jesus said, "Peace be with you!
As the Father has sent me, I am sending you"

– *(John 20:21)* –

Jesus was the light of the world... 'when he was in the world' (John 9:5), but he also referred to the disciples as the light of the world (Matt. 5:14-16). The concept of close partnership seems inescapable, and in Acts 1:1-2 Luke describes the work of Jesus right through to

1: This statement could be twisted to propose the value of self-flagellation or deliberately to put oneself in the way of suffering. At one level all who live a godly life will suffer, but it should not be taken to mean that all of life is suffering! This was not true of Jesus, nor of Paul. I consider rather that there is work to be done and when the body of Christ pursues her mission that there will be opposition, persecution and suffering that is experienced. The intensity of this will vary from epoch to epoch and from one geography to another.

the Ascension as what Jesus 'began' to do and teach. This seems a very appropriate prologue to his second volume, with Luke's Gospel being phase 1 of what Jesus did and taught, and the unfinished second volume (Acts) being the continuation of that same work, phase 2. I write that Acts is a record of the unfinished phase 2 work as it continues and will do so until the *parousia*. We can see the close of the first phase of Jesus' work taking place in Jerusalem with his death and the triumphant claim that it was finished; Acts though does not close with the death of Paul, but in the same fashion as Jesus taught from the Law and the Prophets concerning the kingdom of God in the final chapter of Luke's Gospel and in the first chapter of Acts, so Paul was doing in Rome, in the final chapter of the book.[2]

Jesus had stated that no prophet could die outside Jerusalem and that understanding was a strong element in driving Jesus to that city (Luke 13:31-35). The city that was called to be at the heart of a prophetic people had so sunk that it was the city that now 'stoned and killed the prophets'. There had to be a death for the 'Jew first' so that there could be an unlocking for the world. In the same way that Jesus set his face to travel to Jerusalem (Lk. 9:51), so Paul was resolute that he was on his way to Rome. Ostensibly to give an account to Caesar but I suspect he had in his mind that it was the hour for Caesar to give an account to heaven! The second phase does not end in a death for sins, but through conflict and suffering it involves a message of repentance (a mind shift) about the present state of things and holding out hope for the future.

Israel and Rome

We think of 'church' as a New Testament word, but it has a background that predates that I think is important to explore. It occurs in the Greek translation of the Hebrew Scriptures known as the Septuagint (LXX), the Greek translation that was in common

2: Luke 24: 25-27, 44-49; Acts 1:3; 28:23.

use in the NT era, and the one that is often the basis for the Old Testament quotes. In this important Greek translation *'ekklesia'* is normally the word used to translate the Hebrew word *'qahal'*; this Hebrew word refers to Israel as a people, but specifically Israel as a people called to hear and then to act on the basis of what God had spoken. Outside of that call to purpose another Hebrew word, *'edah'*, was normally used to refer to the people of Israel. The underlying thought seems to be that Israel was *ekklesia* when they were actively responding with purpose.

We also have in the NT a reference to Israel being the 'church/ ekklesia' when they were in the wilderness. In response to God's deliverance, they were on the journey through the wilderness to the 'promised land'. We read:

Moses was in the assembly in the wilderness.

– *(Acts 7:38)* –

('assembly' being the word 'ekklesia')

We will therefore get some idea as to what lies behind the word 'church' if we consider the call of Israel. Interestingly after Israel is taken into captivity in Babylon, a fresh system developed for the religious life of the nation, that of the synagogue. The weekly meeting with a focus on the 'law, prophets and writings' kept Israel focused in an alien land. There was a move away from the cycle of festivals, and the sacrifices to a regular local meeting place. The NT does not base its description of the people of Messiah on that terminology.[3]

There is though a - perhaps more significant background - from within the political world of Paul's day and it is to that I will turn.

3: James 2:2 could be used to suggest that 'synagogue' language is also used (someone comes into your 'synagogue'). This is not the norm of Scripture, it is in the book of James which is more Jewish than the Pauline writings, and what the concept was meant to suggest is not easy to discern.

In brief, I will first summarise the political world that the New Testament was written within.

Rome: one size fits all

The one time we have had an-all but one-world government was the world of the New Testament. Rome's rule extended beyond anything that had gone before. It is for this reason that I see no reason to posit a future one-world government, nor a global antiChrist. The birth context of the church was challenging, and whenever we lose 'faith' perhaps we should consider the historical background where our faith began. Opposition was the norm and yet also a gradual expanding influence was experienced, though that influence did not lead to the message of 'follow Jesus and he will give you a nice life to fit your plan'.

The Roman world was the empire of its day. For the Jews, the big 'monster' had been Babylon (before that, Egypt, and post-Babylon, it was Greece) and from the time of the Babylonian exile and domination, Babylon continued to symbolically represent the enemy of Israel. Hence the term 'Babylon' could be applied concretely to Rome, being the empire of the day and the ongoing symbol for that one-world opposition to the kingdom of God.

The Pax Romana

In true Imperial fashion, Rome conquered and offered a way of life beyond anything that had gone before. The 'Pax Romana' spread across the world - a peace that came through the power of the sword. Comply and be blessed; resist and be eliminated! Paul's words concerning the powers being appointed by God and that they can wield the sword are so tongue in cheek given Nero's claim that he did not need to raise the sword. What a man of peace Nero was... NOT!

Peace in the imperial world was considered such an achievement that the one who brought it (the Emperor) was seen to be operating with divine power. This would increasingly point toward the divine nature of the emperor.

However, this peace was not the absence of war, it was the result of war, as peace meant being in submission to Rome. Peace was imposed on the subjugated by means of force. Peace was brought about by taking lives and creating inequality. The Pax Romana!

As is often the case, the reality is there to be seen if we are willing to look. The altar of peace stood on Mars Hill, the hill dedicated to the god of war! Peace was brought about through the war that the Romans armies fought to subdue all other peoples.

The contrast to the message of Jesus is startling. He established peace through sacrifice, not through killing his enemies. It was love for the enemy that was exhibited at the cross; thus all powers were stripped bare and unmasked. The lie exposed.

Caesar was indeed 'lord and saviour' and 'king of kings'

In secular Greek, the word 'saviour' was attributed to someone who had done something significant that safeguarded the people or preserved what was precious. That person 'saved' the city, and as a result, such activity could earn a person the title of saviour. Not surprisingly the very title 'saviour' was in common use for the Roman emperor, especially denoting his ability to maintain or restore peace in the empire.

Of Julius Caesar, it was written:

In addition to these remarkable privileges
they named him father of his country,

stamped this title on the coinage, voted to celebrate his birthday by public sacrifice, ordered that he should have a statue in the cities and in all the temples of Rome, and they set up two also on the rostra, one representing him as the saviour of the citizens and the other as the deliverer of the city from siege, and wearing the crowns customary for such achievements.

– *(Dio 44.4.5)* –

Likewise, in connection to Augustus:

Whereas the Providence which has guided our whole existence and which has shown such care and liberality, has brought our life to the peak of perfection in giving to us Augustus Caesar, whom it filled with virtue for the welfare of mankind, and who, being sent to us and to our descendants as a saviour, has put an end to war and has set all things in order.

– *(Priene calendar inscription; 9 B.C.)* –

The emperor was often called 'the saviour of the world' or 'the saviour of the inhabited earth'.

It is not surprising that on hearing the apostolic message, people, when seeking to understand it, heard it politically and understood it to be a rebellious message at that. These apostles were proclaiming a rival to Caesar.[4] The message was political. It might even have been possible to miss the deeply spiritual element within it! Yet there is a deep spirituality, a radical relationship to heaven that was contained within it. From that commitment to the God of heaven (the 'foreign'

4: Another example is with the word 'kingdom'. Paul proclaimed the *basileia* (kingdom) of God; the common Greek entitlement for the Roman empire was the *basileia* of Rome.

God of the Jews) this message called for a political way of life and carried a political message for the nations.[5]

If Caesar is not lord, but Jesus is (Lord); if he is not the saviour of the world, but Jesus is; if he is not king of kings, but Jesus is, then we have a clash. The Christian message could be ignored, sidelined, or controlled, but it was certainly no longer a message to an obscure middle eastern people. What Jesus began right through to the days of his Ascension, and Paul's ministry symbolised in his 'ekklesiastical' work will continue 'until he comes'. Indeed the very term 'until he comes' evokes another Imperial concept! We live in a different context and have individualised the message. We have stripped it of its political dynamism and over spiritualised its content.

I cheekily, but deliberately used the word 'ekklesiastical' in the previous paragraph of the apostolic work of Paul. We have Anglicised the word (ecclesiastical) and understand that to be 'church' related work. It is time to look more full on at the very word 'ekklesia'. What was Paul planting? What was his *ekklesiastical* work?

Another Caesar... another *ekklesia*?

It is easy to see how the proclamation was understood to be of 'another Caesar'. To understand the message that way was to reduce it, but not totally misunderstand it. Likewise, in using the term 'ekklesia', we come up against another provocative element that results from the apostolic work.

We can say that Paul was planting churches *(ekklesias)*,[6] but maybe more accurately he was planting a rival *ekklesia*, a rival to the one that

---

5: By political we should not think along the lines of a political party, but a vision for the future of the world. *Polis*, was the Greek word for 'city', and politics was about the shaping of the life of the city-(state).

6: Strictly *ekklesiai*, I have Anglicised the plural by adding a final 's'.

Rome had established there. In the cities where Paul travelled and worked there already was an *ekklesia* present, long before he opened his mouth, and before anyone responded to the proclamation of the Lordship of Jesus. We can see this in the context of the riot in Ephesus. Eventually, the city clerk managed to get the crowd to listen and he said that any complaint had to be dealt with in the proper way, and they should bring it to the 'legal assembly' (Acts 19:39). The two words translated here are the 'legitimate [authorised by Roman decree] *ekklesia*'. Ephesus had a church/*ekklesia*. Paul was planting something there with the same name as that which Rome had endorsed; Ephesus had an ekklesia of Rome, but Paul came to ensure it had an *ekklesia* of Jesus.

It would be very difficult to hear the word 'ekklesia' and to strip it of all its political overtones; I do not consider it was possible for the citizens to make the mental adjustment and to spiritualise it. The word was too potent and well-known. Indeed given how strongly spiritual life ran through the Empire, with Imperial culture indeed being the culture approved of by the gods, the very fact that Paul was proclaiming 'about Jesus and the resurrection' would not have diminished the concept that he was talking politically. Rather it would have simply further emphasised the political nature of the Gospel.

The *ekklesia* (origins in Athens)

The earliest record we have for the 'ekklesia' is from 621BC in Athens, and it was the meeting of all the males who were over 18 years of age and qualified. The meeting had final control over policy, to hear appeals, elect magistrates and confer privileges on individuals. Decision making was by vote, and the opportunity was present to speak up with those over 50 years old being privileged to speak first. Such 'ekklesias' existed in and through the various Greek city-states and carried over in the Roman imperial system, though under Rome's rule it became increasingly a servant of the state. Under either system, it was there to give political shape to the city.

When Paul came to the city, he quickly called the group of disciples an *ekklesia* whose task was to ensure that the kingdom of God was expressed there. A further example of Imperial language, and of how we have lost the context, hence the political implications of following Christ can be seen in Philippians 3:

But our citizenship is in heaven.
And we eagerly await a Saviour from there,
the Lord Jesus Christ, who, by the
power that enables him to bring
everything under his control,
will transform our lowly bodies so that
they will be like his glorious body.

Therefore, my brothers and sisters,
you whom I love and long for, my joy and crown,
stand firm in the Lord in this way, dear friends!

– *(Phil 3: 20-4:1)* –

Removed from the Imperial context it can quickly be used to inspire a song such as, 'This world is not my home, I am just a passing through...', or a theology of 'saved to go to heaven'. But, and thank God there is a but!

Rome was attractive, and all roads led to that glorious city. Many Roman citizens were drawn to move there, but this presented an enormous problem as the infrastructure, the water and sewerage systems could not cope with a growing population. This brought about a very smart policy. Rome could give citizenship to those who lived elsewhere (e.g. Philippi), and they could pride themselves in being Roman citizens. They might live in Philippi, a Greek city, but their citizenship was in Rome. As citizens, they were not to get on the road to Rome but were called to be responsible to ensure that the culture of Rome was present where they lived. It might be tough and counter-culture in seeking to establish Rome's norms in a Greek city such as Philippi, but they could call for help from Rome, and they all looked forward to the day of the arrival *(parousia)* of the Emperor when any doubt of who was 'lord' would be squashed.

Paul's language is explicitly drawing on Imperial language and concepts and far from encouraging them to think 'this world is not my home' his words exhorted them not to get on the road to heaven but to 'stand firm' as citizens of heaven. Tough times might be here, but they can call for help from heaven, and one day... one day there will be the *parousia*[7] of all *parousias.*

'Let your kingdom come' (on earth) is the ongoing prayer and sets the context for the political task ahead. The work of Christ is indeed unfinished. The Imperial context and Pauline language makes that clear. The church as 'movement' is indeed central, not periphery.

7: The Scriptures speak of the *parousia* of Christ (in popular language termed the 'Second Coming'. It was a common place word, but became attached as an Imperial term, meaning literally 'arrival' or 'presence' and with reference to the Emperor's visit to a city. I use it rather than 'second coming' or some other term so that we do not simply force it to conform to a predetermined concept such as we might have of the 'second coming'.

CHAPTER 2

AUTHORISED LABEL

The *ekklesia* in each city carried legitimate authority as it was there to outwork the Roman agenda. There are many writings that seek to legitimise one form of church over another. This might be through a claim to apostolic succession or via denominational legitimation, but I am more focused on the common adjective that once placed in front of the noun seems to carry weight. It is the adjective 'local'. If a church is 'local' it is legitimate; if somehow trans-local, then it is often deemed 'para'-church, something that is not really church but sits alongside church. Those who are part of a para-church movement are often required to show that they are in some way accountable to the local church.[1]

In most Protestant circles, the adjective 'local' has been added to the word 'ekklesia' which seems to give legitimacy to what is being expressed... the trouble is that, by default (or design), all other expressions seem to be declared as illegitimate, or only semi-legitimate. The adjective 'para' once added, does indicate that

1: Accountability is an elusive factor. Being part of something does not mean anyone is accountable, indeed some of the tightest structures have been proven inadequate as far as ensuring that those who represent those structures comply with the accepted behaviour. A structure might or might not aid accountability, but the reality is that accountability is a relational not structural term. Accountability is voluntary.

they have some relationship to church, but seems to insinuate that what is being described is not fully the real thing.

The so-named New Church Movement is what shaped me with a belief that the church was built on a foundation laid by apostles and prophets. The ongoing work of the church was to evangelise a locality, plant new *LOCAL* expressions that carried the same DNA as the mother expression, and enable people to grow in Christ. And I thank God for the many lives that have been impacted through that work.

I can certainly find the understanding of the church in the locality ('saints in Corinth', for example), and the use of the word 'church' across a region (Acts 9: 31), but there does not seem to be the actual sanctifying of that adjective 'local'. In challenging the use of that adjective I am not questioning the validity of a local expression, but I present the challenge in order to open up the possibility that other expressions of the body of Christ can be legitimised. If there is a liberating aspect of focusing on the body of Christ as a living organism and missional body, then we have to challenge the exclusive use of applying the term church only to one specific expression.

Unless we suggest that Jesus' use of the word 'ekklesia' in Matthew 18:17 are words written back into the mouth of Jesus by the writer, then he seemed to suggest that the travelling companions were indeed church... and certainly not 'local'.

If they still refuse to listen, tell it to the church (ekklesia);
and if they refuse to listen even to the church,
treat them as you would a pagan or a tax collector.

If Jesus saw the disciples as 'church', it would be in line with the Septuagint (the Greek translation of the 'Old Testament' in use in Jesus' era) using the term *ekklesia* for the people on mission, travelling to their destiny.

Back to Paul. So, what was he up to? He borrowed terms that were understood, and either ran the risk of people misunderstanding his terminology or more likely, wanted his choice of words to confront the supposed reality that shaped everyday life. He carried an alternative vision for the world. The core of the *ekklesia* of God was made up of those who were from the 'not many' part of society.

> *Not many of you were wise by human standards; not many were influential; not many were of noble birth.*
>
> – *(1 Cor. 1:26)* –

It is probably not surprising that it was not the elite who responded as they were the ones who benefited from the then-current social order, and for them perhaps the 'gospel' was not perceived as good news. Yet the choice of the nobodies was in order to 'to nullify the things that are', and to 'shame the wise' and the 'strong'. The culture was based around a very fixed honour/shame basis. The elite were to be honoured; others were shamed in the sense of knowing their right submissive place. Those chosen by God might not fit in too well to the successful world of the Roman elite, but their humble background and status meant they were a good fit for the radical *ekklesia*.

The Imperial terminology and the Pauline terminology might have been parallel, but the core ethos was so different. All Imperial structures ultimately were there to serve the centre. In the Imperial world of Rome, there could be other 'kings', but Rome would always remain as the 'city that rules over the kings of the earth' and Caesar would continue unchallenged as 'king of kings'. Centres other than Rome could develop, but they would always remain subservient to the main centre. Such centres could only have carefully delegated and monitored authority, certainly no authority was ever distributed. The body of Christ was so different. The goal of the *ekklesia* of Jesus was to truly empower everyone so that one and all could engage in works of service.[2]

If the *ekklesia* of Jesus was to truly shape the city according to a heavenly culture, it is very hard to deny the right to use the term 'church' to any group of people in relationship to Jesus who are focused on working toward redemptive change coming to their 'city'; conversely, it is also quite difficult to give the word *ekklesia* to any group of those who want to use the term *ekklesia* in a way that only legitimises themselves, and certainly if they themselves are not outworking what it means to be an *ekklesia*.

Bring on the apostles

In the West, we are now at the end of an extended Christendom era.[3] Perhaps we are currently alive at a time that will be viewed as the biggest shift in the civilisation of humanity. An apostolic manifestation is always needed whenever there is a shift. We might never actually know what on earth Paul was doing, but we will certainly have to figure out between us all what on earth we are to do! And if our focus does not carry at some level a political element with a vision for a transformed society, it will be very hard to show

2: The vision that Paul outlines in Ephes. 4: 11-13 is of the building up of the body. The ministry gifts were established for the body, not to establish the ministry gifts. In another passage he says that all gifts belong to the body; churches do not belong to the 'apostle'.

3: Christendom can be understood as a period in society when not only certain values were present to shape the wider context, but that a privileged relationship between church (as upholders of societal / state affairs) and the state (giving protection and privilege to the church) existed to mutual benefit. The conversion of Constantine (312AD) is what gave birth to this relationship. Prior to that era Christians were marginalised and very few served in the military world, for example. They did not see their role as upholding the state. Post that time a 'Christian' (Christendom) value was that of defending the state, and this defence of the state was often seen as a defence of the kingdom of God. The language of 'The holy Roman Empire' might be extreme but highlights the conflation of the 'kingdom of God' to that of an earthly structure and geography. Such concepts continue with language such as 'Christian nation', or the, greatly taken out of context, suggestion that there are 'sheep' and 'goat' nations.

that our message is faithful to the one Paul received from heaven.[4]

The apostolic of every generation or situation has to rework the application of the Gospel without ever changing the Gospel itself. If we want to be faithful we will have to renounce hierarchy, be personally upended and immersed in the soil. Years ago, I discovered a strange piece of art. It was of a church, complete with traditional steeple, planted upside down into the ground. A little research and it became clear that it was chosen deliberately and certainly not as something anti-ecclesiastical. The creation was termed 'the device to root out evil'. What a choice of imagery! An upside-down church planted in the soil to root out evil. If the world is to be turned upside down the imagery was indeed appropriate. We should and must ask some deep questions such as 'Could there be a people who are called to root out evil? Could that be possible?' Even if that is going too far, we need to be influenced by those who are intoxicated with the Pauline gospel who rise up (and therefore also go down deep) and help us entertain the thought that the church is much more than a private club but a wonderful 'device' in the plan of God to root out evil.

Laying on one side who can legitimately use the term 'church' I consider that it is vital that the call of *ekklesia* is responded to. Maybe we will all find ourselves in settings that are 'sub-church'! Now there is an adjective ('sub') that might be very applicable. 'Local sub-church', 'para-sub-church'. We would all benefit from taking a step down, for there is a mission to fulfil not a title to claim. I find the thought of what on earth was Paul up to in planting and nurturing *ekklesias* within the one-world government system of Rome not only fascinating but immensely challenging.

4: These thoughts carry big concept language. All of which has to be put into the practical language of 'me', 'my neighbour' etc. The concepts might be large, the activity wonderfully small.

In a very real way, Jesus (and no one else could have done this) opened the door for Peter[5] to give shape to what an *ekklesia* would be within the Jewish world. Peter was the 'apostle to the Jew'. That gives us one window on *ekklesia*, but that window opens to the world of pre-70AD and also of pre-Gentile mission. That is not our world, and it is really the expression of *ekklesia* beyond that that should provoke us to think deeper. Jesus opened the door for Peter; Peter subsequently opened the door for Paul, in that he (Peter) was the first, and reluctantly at that, to go beyond the Jewish world to the Gentiles. The Gentiles (us lot) were Paul's first-century mission field. The context was not of a covenant-people but of the world, and, as already mentioned, an all-but one-world government world. Paul described himself as an apostle to the Gentiles, his task being to take the message of the crucified Jewish Messiah into that culture. He could not change the Gospel, but he had to work out the application of the eternal Gospel into a new context; hence there is the need for an apostolic gift in every new situation and into every new generation. What if the door that Paul went boldly through remains open and we need to go through it into the vastly different world(s) that has/have developed.

The signs of an apostle were with Paul, he claimed in 2 Corinthians 12:12, yet the signs he quotes of the miraculous would not prove sufficient to be recognised by Jesus (Matt. 7:21, 22). However, there was another element Paul added to his credentials. Miraculous signs **and** great patience. A truly apostolic vision focuses on a work within a generation but also has a longer-term vision that works now for future generations. I consider that, in spite of the enormity of the task, Paul genuinely considered that by planting Jesus-shaped *ekklesias* across the Roman world, the system could be changed. That is a political vision; that is an apostolic vision. Anything less does not seem to be a vision suitable for the *ekklesia*.

5: Peter, as representative of the next generation of Jewish believers much more than Peter as a unique person.

There is good research that shows that many forms of church enable people to grow to a level of faith, but then by default, place a ceiling over people going further. We also know of many lone-rangers who seem to get detached from the core of the faith. As I look at the wider world, we are in crisis. We could see the collapse of so much, or the coming together in alliances that provide the platform for dictators. Into that context, I cannot help but believe Paul's Gospel is so relevant. And yes, I do think he was pushing the movement end of the spectrum, while strongly recognising how much we need one another.

This chapter might have seemed a little bit of an attack on 'local', but it was not intended as such, and I consider we have to try and re-align any vision we have of church to the apostolic vision that Paul embodied.[6] I don't consider that vision was formed simply by the world of Imperial Rome but was deeply shaped by the whole purpose of Israel's commission, and before there was an Israel, humanity's commission. The very reason for the existence of the human race was the foundation for Paul's vision of ekklesia. This is not surprising as we maybe could even translate Jesus, the 'last Adam', as 'Adam - at last'. In partnership together, Jesus and the woman from his side.

6: 'Fit for purpose' is what comes to mind. Whatever our views on how the Christian community is formed our relating together should facilitate the appropriate purpose. Sadly, in many settings and over years the outer form is maintained and defended at all costs with little attention being given to the vital question as to whether the form is continuing to serve the missional purpose. Once we accept that any 'form' is provisional and that no group of believers will fulfil the entire apostolic vision we do not need to be very critical of what is on the landscape, other than seeking to be self-critiquing.

CHAPTER 3

STEP UP TO THE PLATE

Once we move beyond the science of how the world came into being and approach the theological 'why?' questions posed by Genesis, we can begin to see the purpose of *ekklesia* within that bigger picture. If we do not engage in that way, we can fall back to the small vision of 'tickets out of here to heaven'. The big framing questions are the 'why' questions. Questions such as 'Why creation?' And even more relevantly 'Why humanity?'

I am comfortable to use the language of 'fallen' when referring both to humanity and also to creation, indicating that both are now below what they were intended to be or to become. Creation has fallen only because of humanity's fall, not voluntarily, but due to the connection between humanity and creation, following by way of necessity. We also can project forward and note that new creation will follow the establishment of a new humanity. Jesus, in his resurrection becoming the first of a new humanity, but also the firstborn of all creation. Creation follows where humanity travels - true, past and future.

Although I believe 'fallen' is an appropriate term for creation as we now have it, perhaps a better image might be that of a woman who has not yet given birth. She is groaning and suffering labour pains

(Rom. 8:22) waiting for liberation.[1] Humanity (Adam and Eve if you like) were appointed as stewards of creation. The command to 'rule' (Gen. 1:28) has to be understood as a commission to serve and care for creation (Gen. 2: 5,15). There is nothing in these early texts that suggest humanity was empowered to dominate over in any exploitative sense; indeed, the text seems to suggest that humanity's role was to bring creation to a mature future. From the beginning, creation was declared 'good', but this does not imply perfect.

It is possible that the Adam and Eve stories functioned in Israel not so much as a story of human origins but of Israel's origins, with the garden of Eden paralleling the land flowing with milk and honey. Certainly, the first 11 chapters sit together as a backdrop for the Abraham and nation of Israel story, either by way of a quick parallel or as the backstory. In those early chapters a path is presented, either for blessing or for curse to come. Without the intervention of God, it seems inevitable that there will only be one outcome, an increasing manifestation of the reality of curse and alienation.

God does intervene (Genesis 12) with the call of Abraham. Through this intervention, blessing will flow from heaven and as a result to the world, and that blessing will flow to the world through the nation of Israel. Israel's election is not one of 'saved' to 'damn all others' but chosen in order to bless all others.

The Adam and Eve story tells us that they did not step up to the plate but became consumers. The 'we are blessed so you can be blessed' became 'we are blessed so now we will consume for ourselves yet more', and later this becomes the same story in Israel.

1: The concept of creation being destroyed is not something the biblical narrative feeds but a concept that Greek Platonic philosophy would be happy with. Although to divinise creation would be an error, to gently speak of 'mother earth' is not too far from the mark as we all came forth from the dust of the earth. Biblical passages which do speak of a destruction are apocalyptic in nature, and for example 2 Peter 3:6 can happily say that the former earth was destroyed by the flood. It is not speaking of a literal destruction, but a radical difference between the 'before' and the 'after'.

A Royal Priesthood

In Exodus 19: 5,6 we read,

> *Now if you obey me fully and keep my covenant, then out of all nations you will be my treasured possession. Although the whole earth is mine, you will be for me a kingdom of priests and a holy nation. These are the words you are to speak to the Israelites.*

Election, elected as a unique people, a holy nation, a kingdom (but without an earthly sovereign). Why the election as corporate 'priests'? One might suggest they were chosen as priests for God, to minister to him, but it seems there is a key with the phrase 'although (for) the whole earth is mine'. The NIV translation uses the word 'although' but numerous translations use the word 'for', giving purpose to the calling. This is not a call to be separate, but the indication that Israel is called to be in a unique relationship to God for the sake of the world.

> *Even in this tradition in which Israel thinks mostly about itself, we see on the horizon that Israel has an agenda other than its own well-being: the life of the world. The priestly function is to make well-being and healing in the world possible.*[2]

As per many Scriptures, how we read them is in our control. We can read it as 'special and excluding others' or as 'unique to include others'. I have to read it as the latter; all nations are to be blessed through these people. This follows on from the Adamic call, and the context is of Israel having left Egypt and now having arrived at Mount Sinai where they receive the ten words that will shape them

2: *Theology of the Old Testament*, Walter Brueggemann, Augsburg Fortress, Minneapolis, 1977, p. 431.

as a nation (and these ten words are in direct contrast to the values of Egypt).

A very special relationship is on offer, a covenant not of equal partners, but one that has both purpose and conditions. What makes this call all the more powerful is the setting – they have been delivered from their slavery to the Empire and have been wonderfully set free with a unique identity, but the identity clearly does not make it all about them. As a priesthood, they are there to offer sacrifices to God, but there is a significantly deeper role, that of intercession (and by using this word I am using it in the fuller sense of standing in a 'between' or 'on behalf of' role). Their unique identity is to position them for the wellbeing of the world, to make healing possible among the nations.

Even in relation to Egypt we have the irony of Pharaoh, the ruler of vast territory of lands, asking that Jacob, the landless one, bless him (Gen. 47:7); even the later Pharaoh who was the nemesis of Israel asks Moses to bless him as the people get ready to leave their slavery (Exod. 12:32)! The nations need Israel and need her blessing.

The original call of Abraham is in relation to the nations for we read of the nations being blessed through Abraham. Israel cannot live in a vacuum as a chosen people; they are set within the nations as a priesthood for those other peoples. The nations themselves are a result of the fall(s) that are outlined from Gen. 3-11, and the genesis of the chosen people (Gen. 12) in Abraham is for the implicit purpose of releasing them from curse.

We have in the Isaianic passages the servant visions that we clearly see are nation oriented (e.g. Is. 42:6; 49:6). There we read that they are to be a 'covenant to the people' and 'a light to the nations'. The well-being of the nations is Israel's responsibility. Hence, the implicit purpose that is present in the early Genesis chapters becomes explicit here in Exodus 19 and again in Isaiah.

If we read this as the raison d'être for the covenant, we will then read the ongoing story of the people as falling short of that call. Even the 'high' points that are recounted from David's kingship (and a king as a high point has to also be questioned) has to be set against the effect of his son Solomon who begins the systematic enslaving of the nation. The wisdom of Solomon is deeply compromised as he restructures Israel along a highly centralised model. Post-Solomon the result is the split of the nation, with the first king to rule over the northern kingdom (Jeroboam) coming up from Egypt to reign and promptly erecting two golden calves (1 Kings 12). (The resonances with the former history of a people coming up from Egypt and creating a golden calf are sounding very loud when one reads of the kingdoms dividing.) Yes, the northern tribes are in rebellion against the house of David, but there is also a deep relativity that runs through it all. A 'pro-house-of-David and anti-rebellious-northern-tribes' perspective might draw the line of evil along the north/south divide, but there is something deeper going on. Those northern kingdoms might be in rebellion, but Israel, even as idealised in Judah, is also herself deeply fallen. Sadly, the nations and even the northern kingdom are now enemies to be defeated or at least to be separate from.

A high call is placed on humanity (the Adam/Eve story) and on Israel (Abraham and nation story). Their responsibility is the world.

Surely this element lay behind Paul's thoughts as he planted an *ekklesia*. As a formerly trained Pharisee, troubled by the disobedience of Israel, he began to see that far from God's promises having failed, that the line of Abraham was not one of physical descent but of faith, and that this faith was no longer even dependent on Torah obedience. Previously the hope was in one people, a faith people who were nationally inscribed but who had failed. Yet God's plan of redemption for the world had not failed. Taking on Israel's (and therefore Adam's) failure, the Messiah made possible for there to be one corporate people, irrespective of race, no longer defined along the ethnic divide of Jew and Gentile. This one people called to be that holy nation and royal priesthood.

CHAPTER 4

WE NEED A PRIESTHOOD

Once Israel loses sight of the servant role of being a blessing to the nations, there is a gradual fall away from the effective call to be a royal priesthood. A first step is an exchange from being a priesthood for the world to that requiring a priestly tribe for the special nation. Rather than the nation serve the nations, the priesthood will now serve the nation. This marks the pivotal shift that drastically alters the identity of the people and inevitably reduces their vision of God's redemptive activity. With this change, there is the beginning of a fall from the original calling.

As the history of Israel unfolds, there is a downward trajectory that can be tracked where the nation moves away from her original God-given call. That call was in relation to the wider world and the other nations; however, Israel becomes increasingly insular and separate from the nations and ironically in the process becomes more like the other nations. This trajectory 'down' or 'away' from the original purpose is one that has to be and will be in Jesus, reversed. When we consider God as redeemer, we realise that he does not rubbish our activities but, at great personal cost, pulls whatever can be redeemed through not only to the original point but beyond.

This downward movement can be tracked:

- Israel no longer responding as a 'royal priesthood' for the whole earth, and
- with this subtle shift, the desire to 'be like the nations' develops. The result is the big vision picture is reduced, and a priesthood is developed that is for the nation (Israel) rather than the nation acting corporately as a priest for the nations.
- This is solidified when they call for a king, which ultimately was a rejection of God not of Samuel.
- The king has in his heart to build the Temple.

A few observations

God does not disappear when Israel loses her calling; indeed, his glory is even seen in the Temple when it is dedicated. This should be a challenge for us: the presence of God does not validate the setting where he is present.

One of the first demonstrations that result from the Cross is that of tearing the Temple curtain. The Temple being the final manifestation of the downward trajectory it becomes also the first issue touched through the Cross to reverse that trajectory. If the Temple disappears, religion is impacted. We can observe the reaction to Stephen in Acts 7 when he brings up that God does not live in a house made for him. They have reluctantly listened to his impassioned speech to that point, but as soon as he hits the centre-point of the Temple, they quickly move forward to stone the 'blasphemer'. If they accept his point on the Temple, the rest of his speech then gains traction with great personal cost to the listeners. He had been consistently making the point that God was in the habit of revealing himself outside the promised land. The New Testament radically reforms the understanding of 'temple'.

John's words, 'I saw no temple', in Revelation relating to the vision of the New Jerusalem are very powerful. The ripped curtain signifies the end of the Temple and the beginning of a process, the goal of which is the restoration of a people living as a royal priesthood among the nations and for the nations.

Matthew's Gospel which has such a focus on the fulfilment of Scripture, with numerous quotes, seems to start with an allusion to the first book of the Jewish canon. In Matthew 1:1 we read,

A record of the genealogy
(literally 'the genesis') of Jesus Christ.

And he finishes his Gospel with what we term the Great Commission.

Then Jesus came to them and said,
"All authority in heaven and on earth has
been given to me. Therefore go and make disciples
of all nations, baptising them in the name of the
Father and of the Son and of the Holy Spirit,
and teaching them to obey everything I have
commanded you. And surely I am with you always,
to the very end of the age."

The words of the Great Commission surely echo the concluding words of the close of the Jewish 'writings', the book we term 2 Chronicles. There we read the words of King Cyrus,

The Lord, the God of heaven, has given me all the
kingdoms of the earth and he has appointed me to
build a temple for him at Jerusalem in Judah.
Any of his people among you may go up, and may
the Lord their God be with them.

– *(2 Chron. 36: 23)* –

Matthew's Gospel with its many quotes seems to be appropriately wrapped in the entire Hebrew Scriptures with the final commission being of Temple building, but with such a difference. 2 Chronicles has Cyrus calling for the re-building of the Temple in Jerusalem; Jesus likewise is directing the disciples to a building project. A temple not located somewhere but distributed everywhere is what Jesus mandated. A temple where God dwells and as it grew the nations would be discipled. Truly a house of prayer for the nations, a place where the wisdom of heaven could be dispersed and where people could meet the living God. But that is to get ahead of myself.

Reversing the trajectory

Central to the developed life of Israel and also to the Old Testament are the offices of priest and king and the centralised focus of worship at the Temple. There were voices that challenged those offices and institutions, or, at least if not directly, challenged the abuses that resulted from how those offices were carried out. Those challenging voices are found in and through many of the prophets. There is, however, a deeper challenge that appears to be intrinsic within the OT pages that presents the triad (of priest, king and Temple) themselves as fallen and therefore not part of the original purpose for the 'nation' of Israel.

If, as we will seek to trace, we are looking at a trajectory that represents an increasing fallenness, there are two aspects that will come out in the trajectory:

1. God does not depart from the people, nor does he simply abandon the institutions that develop. Far from this, he actually appears within the offices and institution. This is not to be taken that he endorses them, but his identification with the people is greater than any judgement on their fallen path. He inhabits the fallen structures and is present to redeem and bless through those structures.

2. The trajectory continues until Israel's very real separation from its calling and destiny is at a level that can be termed 'the fullness of time'. This Pauline phrase that he uses to describe the *kairos* time of the Incarnation is a more significant theological assessment of the time of the Incarnation than simply a pragmatic one. To suggest that the 'fullness of time' is a pragmatic comment on the ease with which the Gospel could spread through such elements as the communication system, the use of the Greek language, the so-called Pax-Romana and the like, is to take the Pauline phrase and separate it from the theological context of enslavement. The fullness of time was when there was a universal enslavement, and in particular when Israel was enslaved (under a curse) meaning that Israel had to be set free so that the promises to Abraham could come into view and find a fulfilment. The Incarnation was into that context, and Paul's words are somewhat explosive:

But when the fullness of time had come,
God sent his Son, born of a woman, born under the law, in order to redeem those under the law, so that we might receive the adoption as children. And because you are children, God has sent the Spirit of his Son into our (variant reading 'your') hearts, crying, 'Abba! Father!' So you are no longer a slave but a child, and if a child then also an heir, through God.

– *(Gal. 4: 4-7)* –

Paul has the language of 'we' and 'you' and when we find those pronouns within the same context, they normally differentiate the Jew from the Gentile, and so we find it here. (There is, as I noted in the quote, also a variant reading of 'your' heart in verse 6.) Jesus is human but also Jewish; he is under the law with a primary purpose of redeeming the Jew. He is the Saviour of the world, but as Jewish Messiah, he comes to set Israel free from her bondage as it is through the foundational Abrahamic covenant that the world will be blessed.

The evidence that the Gentiles ('you') are now also heirs is not that they have submitted to any element of the Jewish law but that they have received the Spirit, and as a result they also are heirs. This becomes very explicit in Ephesians with the insistence that there is now 'one new humanity in place of the two'.[1]

Again in Galatians, we read of the 'we' / 'you' issue being resolved through the death of Jesus. Paul suggests that the death of Jesus on the cross indicates that he took on the curse of the law, thus redeeming 'us', so that the blessing of Abraham might come to the Gentiles (Gal. 3:12-14).

The fullness of time then was a time in the spiritual history of Israel when there was a fullness of bondage that had to be broken so that a full release of the Abrahamic promises for the nations could be made available. It is this trajectory toward bondage that I wish to trace. It is not that God is absent; indeed, he manifests even within the bondage. This can seem ironic, but rather than understanding it as ironic, we have to allow this to challenge our view of God. His presence does not equate his approval of the container in which his presence is experienced (and given that God is not male, the feminine aspects of God certainly do not fit into man-made containers!). This also suggests that we are not looking to find the total absence of God when we are talking of the bondage in Israel, but that the fallenness had arrived at a level where a tipping point had been reached. Also that the entrance of Jesus at that key moment meant the 'powers' could be exposed and dealt with in such a way that through the sacrificial death of Jesus there could be a once-for-all universal release for Israel and for the nations, along with the implication that the old divide was done away with, and Christ becoming the central focus. Those 'in Christ' being the one new humanity.

So to the trajectory that we want to trace, and as a summary, the pathway will take us from:

1: (Ephes. 2:15) and it is that humanity that is being built into a 'holy temple' (2:21).

- The calling of Israel to be unique among the nations but for the nations, as described in the term 'royal priesthood' or 'kingdom of priests'
- To the institution of the Levitical priesthood which subtly prepares the ground for a substitution in the identity of Israel. It shifts the nation from being a corporate priesthood for the nations to having a tribe of priests (Levi) for the nation herself. A shift from 'for the world' to 'for the chosen nation' is set in place with this substitution.
- To the choosing of a king so that Israel might be just as one of the nations.

[At each step the shift increases in magnitude. So no longer a nation for the nations, but a called nation that is all-but-one of the nations. Still unique, yes, in that God does not leave her, but increasingly fallen.]

- The king builds for God a Temple. With this remarkable event, there is an enormous shift from the understanding of Creation as God's Temple to a centralisation (control?) of God's presence located at the centre (holy of holies) of an institution within Israel's capital city of Jerusalem.

The shift to the Levitical Priesthood

In the Exodus 19 passage, Israel's chosenness and uniqueness are underlined, indicating that they are distinct from the nations. They are a nation, but not a nation as the other nations. They uniquely belong to God, but this is not to mean that the other nations are not God's. They too occupy territory, but their territory is within creation and 'the whole earth is mine'. Israel then is called to be a royal priesthood for the world, and there is a downward trajectory that begins as it loses this calling when the Levitical tribe is chosen to be priests for Israel. 'Israel for the nations' is not directly replaced by 'the Levitical priesthood for Israel' but with this move, and what follows from this, we can see a subtle shift in identity. Israel will become less clear in her corporate identity as set within God's world and will focus more on her distinctiveness among the nations as the centre of her identity. As this occurs, she will increasingly see the extent of God's activity ending at her boundaries.

It is in the aftermath of the golden calf incident that we read of the choice of the Levites:

The Levites did as Moses commanded,
and that day about three thousand of the people died.
Then Moses said, "You have been set apart to the Lord
today, for you were against your own sons and brothers,
and he has blessed you this day".

– (Exod. 32:28,29) –

The violence might be (might be??!!) an issue for us, but in context, we have a people (Levites) who were passionate for the fulfilment of the covenant and so were chosen. They were on 'the Lord's side'. (There is a wonderful contrast between this story and the 3000 who lost their lives when Moses came down the mountain and the story of the 3000 who found life when the Spirit came down on the Day of Pentecost. Luke's record is very deliberate, and highlights that the God-trajectory is from judgement to salvation).

The shift from royal priesthood to a priestly tribe is more subtle than an immediate loss of the royal priesthood calling. Perhaps the call to be a corporate royal priesthood for the nations could have continued even with a priestly tribe within the nation. In Numbers 8:16-18, we read that the Levites replaced the choice of the firstborn from the people:

They are the Israelites who are to be given wholly to me.
I have taken them as my own in place of the firstborn,
the first male offspring from every Israelite woman.

> *Every firstborn male in Israel, whether human or animal, is mine. When I struck down all the firstborn in Egypt, I set them apart for myself. And I have taken the Levites in place of all the firstborn sons in Israel.*

It is not clear if the firstborn were intended to be priests within Israel and the Levites took that role, or whether the post-golden calf incident makes the shift as strong as an exchange of royal priesthood to that of a priestly tribe. So in seeking to be fair, I suggest the shift is more subtle than a blatant exchange.

Two aspects that should caution us can be noted:

- We do not need to make absolute decisions that declare something as pure, in the sense of 'it has to be this way and only this way'. Compromise is part of our journey, rather than the idealism that those of us who are of a certain disposition love.
- And secondly, God goes where we go. He anoints the Levites for the task. He travels with and within the downward trajectory.

This then works in two directions, the tension of which needs to be held together: just because God's anointing is present, we must not read that as an endorsement, and even when we compromise, we should not accept any compromise as an acceptable endpoint.

It is often subtle shifts, the acceptance of what is pragmatic, that becomes the doorway through which further shifts take place that are anything but subtle. I remember being present when a strong interchange between a well-known bishop and an Anabaptist took place. The bishop argued that being a member of the House of Lords was a place where there was the God-given opportunity to shape legislation, therefore a 'godly' place. The response was that if the basis of being there was unjust (read for this 'Christendom') then this could not be seen as a 'godly' place. My vote, of course, was with the Anabaptist! This illustrates the journey.

Idealism (we oppose all forms of Christendom) or compromise (I can do good in that position of influence). I think the way forward is not an either/or but one of continual ongoing redemptive compromise – starting where we are but moving forward and upward in the most redemptive way possible.

The shift to the Levitical priesthood might not be a huge step, but it subtly moved the identity and calling of Israel away from being a corporate royal priesthood for all, to being a special nation whose calling separated them from the nations. Later, in Numbers 35, we read that the Levites were to be dispersed throughout the land. They were not given land separate from the other tribes – maybe a picture of what could have been. The ultimate destiny of any 'God-people' is to be dispersed throughout the lands as dispersal throughout is a necessary element in fulfilling a priestly call on behalf of others. This was certainly the situation post-Pentecost with believers living as aliens in the world, living among the peoples.

CHAPTER 5

GIVE US A KING

In the previous chapter, I suggested that there was a subtle shift that took place with the setting up of the Levitical priesthood, and it is subtle shifts that often lead to much more substantial shifts. Although it appears to me that the Levitical priesthood does indeed mark a loss of the corporate royal priesthood understanding, this is not absolutely explicit within Scripture... but when we come to the issue of kingship the shift of identity is very clear. There is nothing subtle about this move!

1 Samuel 8 is the central passage in this monarchical appointment. We read the following,

So all the elders of Israel gathered together and came to Samuel at Ramah. They said to him, "You are old, and your sons do not follow your ways; now appoint a king to lead us, such as all the other nations have".

But when they said, "Give us a king to lead us", this displeased Samuel; so he prayed to the Lord. And the Lord told him: "Listen to all that the people are saying to you; it is not you they have rejected, but they have rejected me as their king.

As they have done from the day I brought them up out of Egypt until this day, forsaking me and serving other gods, so they are doing to you. Now listen to them; but warn them solemnly and let them know what the king who will reign over them will claim as his rights".

– *(1 Sam. 8: 4-7)* –

Nothing subtle there! We read:

- Now appoint for us a king to lead us like all the nations.
- They have not rejected Samuel, but they have rejected God from being king over them.
- God tells Samuel to solemnly warn them and show them the ways of the king who shall reign over them.

A sobering aspect is in the choice of Saul as king. A humble man, seeking to avoid the limelight, who does not look to put himself forward. It is the people who insist on a king who will do things for them (1 Sam. 8:20). The corporate responsibility to be something for the nations is exchanged for a king who will be something for them as a nation. 'We want to be as the nations' is effectively also shorthand for 'and no longer a royal priesthood', or at least it is a significant step away from that identity and calling.

In giving Saul (and those who follow) the status of king, I wonder if there was not within it the 'curse' of title. As Lord Acton said:

Power tends to corrupt,
and absolute power corrupts absolutely.

Corruption is a tendency not an inevitability, but once Israel rejects God, it becomes almost inevitable that there will be an abuse of the people through the appointment of the king. God says, warn them about the ways of the king and the corruption that will come.

In spite of the rejection, God enters into the world of the king and anoints Saul, David, Solomon and those who follow. As one king dies, there is no discussion on 'should we really have a king to be like the other nations?'; any debate has long since gone. Now the question is not over kingship per se but simply concerning who the next king should be. With the establishment of the monarchy, Israel has moved a long way from being there for the nations to being (as) one of the nations. God is still present, he does not disown the people, but as they lose their uniqueness, so they lose the focus and the ability to be a priesthood for the nations.

The king builds a Temple

The Temple in its various manifestations carried great significance for Israel. The building of the second Temple post-exile signified a measure of dignity and autonomy to the people. When, in the period of Greek domination, the Hasmoneans cleansed the Temple in 164BC, it gave them a strong basis of perceived legitimacy to form the Hasmonean dynasty. In the time of Jesus we have the Temple, though not yet complete, built by Herod the Great thus validating his claim to be king of the Jews. The Temple always stood for something, and in the time of Jesus, the obvious grandeur of Herod's Temple communicated something about the uniqueness of this nation, Israel, and God's promise to live with and defend this people.

The original temple, prepared for by David and constructed by his son, Solomon, was a key feature of his reign and legitimised his unique standing before God, as his 'son'. 1 Kings 8 is a chapter where we can pick up on Solomon's Temple:

The priests then brought the ark
of the Lord's covenant to its place in the inner
sanctuary of the temple, the Most Holy Place,
and put it beneath the wings of the cherubim.

The cherubim spread their wings over the place of the ark and overshadowed the ark and its carrying poles. These poles were so long that their ends could be seen from the Holy Place in front of the inner sanctuary, but not from outside the Holy Place; and they are still there today. There was nothing in the ark except the two stone tablets that Moses had placed in it at Horeb, where the Lord made a covenant with the Israelites after they came out of Egypt.

– (1 Kings 8:6-12) –

The Temple filled with the glory of God would seem to validate this move, yet even in the dedication Solomon holds on to a higher truth, 'Even heaven and the highest heaven cannot contain you, much less this house that I have built!' (1 Kings 8:27). I suspect, though, that the building of the impressive Temple did not expand the vision of the people to see God as inhabiting the whole earth, but rather confirmed a perspective that he was present in Jerusalem and within the inner sanctuary of the Temple in a very intense way. The cloud of glory would even seem to endorse this viewpoint.

The Temple, at one level a mere symbol, became the reality to such an extent that it obscured the vision of God present throughout the earth. For this reason, we have to ensure that our purported beliefs and our practice do not conflict. We might proclaim that the earth belongs to the Lord, but once we name a building the 'sanctuary', we should not be surprised that it becomes increasingly difficult to carry the holy presence of God with us.

There is a tension within the narratives. God is present everywhere, but his intense presence is manifest within the Temple. There are continuing tensions we face. God's Temple is creation, and he is depicted as seated within Creation with heaven as his throne and the earth as his footstool. In the Creation narratives humanity is placed, in line with the Ancient Near Eastern understanding of temple imagery, inside the sanctuary as the image of the invisible God. Hence God is present in all places, and yet he is found in an intensified way in specific places. Even a theology of 'home' suggests this, for we cannot impose God in all places, but we can within our own circle invite this God to take up residence with us.

The issue with the Temple was not the tension of the universal and the particular, but that the particular geo-location of the Temple weakened and ultimately cancelled out the universal. Further, it pushed away the identity of Israel, as a unique people, being located to carry representative responsibility within the nations of the earth to a focus on them as the centre, this focus eventually resisting the push outward. Living in a strange land they were not able to sing the songs of Zion, whereas a prophet like Jeremiah who relativised the importance of the Temple provoked them to buy land and seek the welfare of the city – even the welfare of Babylon.

Reading the pages of the OT we are often left hanging in the midst of the debate, and if all we had were those pages, we would find it hard to navigate to a place of clarity. It is, of course, the pages of the NT that we have to turn to, to the ministry of the one true human, the true Israel to find how we should respond to the issues raised in the trajectory. In seeking clarity:

- I suggest that God never desired a priesthood, a monarchy, nor a temple. He did not call for these but worked with these at each step of Israel's journey.
- Within each of the above, the presence of God is discovered. However, we cannot take that presence as endorsing the container in which he is revealed.
- Although he is revealed through and found within those containers, the very containers themselves also in part hide or distort the revelation.

The ultimate direction from Exodus 19 (royal priesthood) to the context we find in the opening pages of the Gospels is not one of fulfilling the calling to be a priesthood for the nations, but of a decreased ability to do so. In the NT context there was an impressive Temple with a priesthood, but that priesthood was deeply compromised with Rome. The compromise can be seen for what it is in John's Gospel. We read there that the chief priests claimed they had no king but the emperor (John 19:15). So much for being a theocracy![1] That same priesthood also saw the death of Jesus as necessary so that they could continue to live comfortably under Rome (John 11: 48-53).

In the NT era, we encounter the dubious king (Herod) whose building project is the Temple. In spite of Rome's rule the three elements of priest, king and temple are all still visible, but the overall sense in the land was one of being in Exile, of being separated from their God in any real sense. The statement in Matthew's Gospel that in Jesus 'God is with us' (Emmanuel) is momentous. In the Incarnation God is returning to the land, but not as one to endorse those three elements as they existed. Jesus' appearance signalled the end of those three institutions as he narrowed the options claiming that 'he was the (unique) way', and that those who spoke against what God was doing by the Spirit would find there was no other way to experience forgiveness, not in this life nor in the age to come.[2]

There had been a downward trajectory, indeed so much so that Paul says that the death of Jesus was to break the curse on Israel. How far

---

1: With this declaration there is a completion of the request in 1 Sam. 8:20 to 'be like the nations' by having a king. Now the confession of Caesar as their king means they are one of the nations. If Israel was to hold back dominating power, perhaps the choosing of a king in 1 Sam. 8 over the priestly nation eventually allowed a 'Caesar' to reign over the world? That world sadly includes Israel, by the time of Jesus. The only slender thread that holds out a distinct hope for Israel is found in the rather complex chapters in Romans (9-11) where Paul maintains that they 'are loved on account of the patriarchs' (11:28).

2: The 'blasphemy against the Holy Spirit'.

was this fall? For the Jew, it was self-evident that the nations (Gentiles) were living under a curse, but those nations were dependent on a truly free Israel in order to find their freedom. Sadly that nation, the one called to be unique, had also become one of the many nations. Here is the deeper significance of Jesus coming in 'the fullness of time', born human, born Jewish to redeem those under the law.

Jesus came to form a people, and there could be no greater symbolic choice than to choose twelve as the foundation. Those followers asked post-resurrection, 'Are you at this time going to restore the kingdom to Israel?' (Acts 1:7) and that question might have been provoked by their inability to envisage a future without a Temple. Perhaps they expected a revived Israel over the nations? Or maybe we are meant to understand the question differently and deeper along the lines of 'are you going to restore the kingdom call of Israel at this time?' Perhaps they were beginning to understand the kingdom consisted of priests who served the interests of others and that it was not a kingdom that exercised rulership over others. Jesus' reply is interesting as he draws together various Isaianic passages, and culminates it with the phrase 'the ends of the earth'. This last phrase surely alluding (and more than alluding) to Isaiah 49:6,

> *It is too small a thing for you to be my servant to restore the tribes of Jacob and bring back those of Israel I have kept. I will also make you a light for the Gentiles, that my salvation may reach to the ends of the earth.*

Likewise, the other Scriptures alluded to in Jesus' reply suggest that this is indeed what he is envisaging. He is not talking about a kingdom being restored as in a nation separate to the nations, but of a people who will indeed be a kingdom of priests. Jesus, rather than answer with a yes/no gives an answer to the deeper issue. This is not about giving Israel back her land with a suitable king, but rather it is of calling a people to whom he will restore the calling to be a kingdom of priests.

A downward trajectory has been what we have looked at. Now through the coming of Christ, the great reversals were to begin. Temple, king and priests have to give way to the One who came, embodying those three elements, but embodying them with a different Spirit. He came to serve in order to include, not to rule and exclude. He came to 'empty' those institutions, to restore a kingdom of priests so as the nations again might be blessed.

CHAPTER 6

THE TEMPLE HAS TO GO

I have been suggesting that the downward trajectory culminates in the building of the Temple. If this is so, then it should not be a great surprise that Jesus does not give the stones that made up the Temple a guarantee beyond the generation of his day.

The 'sacred' Temple the disciples were so impressed by would within a generation be desecrated, left desolate and torn down. The shock of that to the disciples then (and maybe also now to many believers) cannot be overstated.

The Cleansing of the Temple: John's version

John places the cleansing of the Temple at the beginning of his Gospel while the Synoptic Gospels place at the end of the ministry of Jesus. For some, this suggests that there were two cleansings, one at the beginning and one at the end of Jesus' ministry. I do not hold to two cleansings of the Temple, but that viewpoint is incidental.

I consider that John's positioning of the cleansing at the beginning of the ministry of Jesus is not making a chronological but a theological point. So first to John and the early chapters of his Gospel.

'In the beginning' (1:1) carries such a resonance to Genesis, and we have subsequent references to 'the light of the world' paralleling that of 'Let there be light' from the first creation account. The text is full of Creation symbolism, or perhaps we should say New Creation symbolism. We have in the text a succession of days:

- 'the next day' occurs twice (1:29, 1:35): this then accounts for three days of 'creation' (two 'next' days, indicating two days after the opening 'in the beginning' day).
- After that, disciples come and remain with Jesus 'that day' (1:39): a fourth day.
- We then have another reference to 'the next day' (1:43): a fifth day.
- There is no reference to the sixth day, the day when humanity was created – the truly human one is not created.
- After that 'week' has passed, we read of a reference to an event that takes place 'on the third day' (2:1). This, of course, pushes us beyond the Creation narrative and forward to the new creation day/week that will be inaugurated through the resurrection (on the third day).

So, in the above 'days', we have a movement in a week with a skipping over of day 6 – Jesus is not simply a new 'adam' with the breath of God in him, but he is the word made flesh... He is not simply humanity with the breath of God inside being drawn ever-Godward, but he is God attracted forever humanward. The narrative recalibrates creation and the wedding at Cana on the third day gives us a window into post-resurrection life. The water for the Jewish rites of purification is changed into the wine that can only be drunk in the new creation. This is described as the first of the signs and through which his glory was revealed (2:12).

We then have a pause and a 'few days' pass with the next event recorded being the Johannine account of the Temple cleansing. This is why I consider John has placed the cleansing right up front. The new creation has to cleanse the Temple, but even more than cleansing the existing Temple - the Temple itself has to give way to the Temple which is his body (2:19).

(Incidentally, the next two sections in John are the visit of Nicodemus, a great teacher of Israel, who needs to be born again, or he will not be able to even 'see' the kingdom of heaven. He comes in the middle of the night. Contrast this with the Samaritan woman who Jesus meets in the middle of the day, and to whom he reveals himself (and she 'sees' him) as the Saviour. Ethnicity, nor gender, will no longer be a sufficient basis to be at the centre).

The Temple cleansing – other accounts

The other accounts place the Temple cleansing where I consider it took place chronologically – in that final week in Jerusalem. The prophet has to die in Jerusalem – that centre is the place that has to be the focus, and we read that Jesus had set his face like flint to go to Jerusalem. Here I might sound a little controversial, but hold with it! It is not the centre with the identity of being the holy city that is calling Jesus. He is not going to Jerusalem on pilgrimage, but going there as the place where the fall from redemptive calling is centred. Break it open there, and there is a break for the world. He is the Jewish Messiah, to fulfil the promises to Israel so that the call to bless the nations can be truly released. He restores this by first breaking the curse over Israel.

I will keep on driving out demons and healing
people today and tomorrow, and on the third day
I will reach my goal. In any case, I must press on today
and tomorrow and the next day - for surely
no prophet can die outside Jerusalem!

Jerusalem, Jerusalem, you who kill the prophets
and stone those sent to you, how often I have longed to
gather your children together, as a hen gathers
her chicks under her wings, and you were not willing.
Look, your house is left to you desolate. I tell you, you will
not see me again until you say, 'Blessed is he who comes
in the name of the Lord'.

– *(Luke. 13:33-35)* –

When he finally comes to Jerusalem, he weeps over the city (Luke 19:41) as he only sees judgement ahead at the hands of the Romans. Having declared what he saw in the city, he makes one further visit, to the Temple. He is looking for something there that is redemptive, that perhaps could even hold back judgement. However, he does not find in the Temple what might have been a slender life-line, for he does not find the Temple as a house of prayer (for all nations) but as a den of robbers. The very Temple has betrayed the calling, compromised over power and money.[1] With that, the bondage is complete, and the tragic future of the Temple is set. Within a generation it will become evident that the Temple is left desolate, but I suspect on that visit Jesus saw that it was already desolate.[2]

In Matthew 24, we read:

Jesus left the temple and was walking away
when his disciples came up to him to call his attention
to its buildings. "Do you see all these things?" he asked.

1: The parallel with Judas can be noted.

2: There is a parallel with the 'cursing' of the fig tree that seems to be linked in Mark's version (Mk. 11:12-25). Jesus sees the fig tree and declares that no-one will eat fruit from the tree again. Then comes the cleansing of the Temple. Upon their return the disciples note that the fig tree had withered. There was a time lapse, but the tree was 'left desolate' when he had visited it and spoke over it. The cleansing of the Temple meant its ultimate desolation. There might be a time lapse of a generation, just as there was a time lapse of a day with regard to the fig tree.

"Truly I tell you, not one stone here will be left on another; every one will be thrown down".

– *(Matt. 24:1-2)* –

Tragic in the eyes of his Jewish disciples, and nothing less than the end of the age. Their question about the end of the age should not be understood as a question about the 'Second Coming' as those asking the question could not even see the Easter events that were about to take place. We cannot take this question therefore along the lines of a standard modern-day Christian perspective concerning the 'Second Coming'.

Seen from a pre-Easter perspective, the Temple destruction was viewed as a disaster, so great that it would be the 'end of the age' (and so it was). That pre-Easter perspective though would have to give way to an incredibly expansive viewpoint of a living temple where God dwells, not located inside stones in a specific location but inside the corporate lives of a unique people distributed everywhere.

The Temple and the early disciples

As much as Jesus was not intrinsically anti-Temple, neither were the early disciples. They continued to gather in that setting in Acts, and Paul went through purification rites within the Temple (Acts 21:26, albeit from following the advice of James). However, there were implications through the death of Jesus for the Temple. Perhaps Stephen who was associating with a more open-minded synagogue (Acts 6:9) was the first one to push hard a point that he repeatedly makes in his speech (Acts 7), namely that the visitations of God were persistently outside the land of Israel. That perspective was what took him to the point he made about the Temple and where God's dwelling place really was. The end result of challenging the legitimacy of the Temple was stoning.

There is, I consider, a clear literary twist of irony in the Lucan account. Those who stoned Stephen laid their coats at the feet of a young man called Saul, who we read explicitly approved of the killing (Acts 8:1). Saul continued his opposition to the new movement by persecuting any Jewish households that were believing Jesus to be the Messiah. The twist though is that after the Damascus encounter and we begin to read the Pauline message we realise that if ever there was a Jew who carried the mantle of Stephen, it was Paul. The coats might be at his feet, but the coat of Stephen would soon be on his shoulders.

Just as we read in John's Gospel that the cleansing of the Temple was on the third day, we will read of a three-day incident for Saul of Tarsus. This time we read of a three-day period of blindness. Paul, blind until he could see that the crucified Jew was crucified not for his own sins, but for the curse on the nation. Stephen had underlined a point that the glory of God was consistently revealed outside the land; likewise, Paul's revelation comes not within the land but within the foreign soil of Damascus!

I consider that either the early church was ambivalent about the Temple in that it no longer carried any redemptive purpose, or as Jews, they were unable to come to terms that its day was over. Whether either of the above is right or not, it seems to me that there was a growing expectation of a great and imminent shift:

By calling this covenant "new,"
he has made the first one obsolete; and what
is obsolete and outdated will soon disappear.

– (Heb. 8:13) –

It will soon disappear! There is no evidence in early Christian writings post-70AD (the destruction of Jerusalem and the Temple) of an expectation of the Temple being rebuilt. The events that climaxed in 70AD with the final collapse and destruction of Jerusalem at the hands of the Romans were seen as the fulfilment of Jesus' words that we read as the Olivet Discourse. If the Temple was one element that contributed to the downward trajectory of Israel, it should not be surprising that those who followed the Messiah understood that they were occupying the space the Temple formerly occupied, but not in the same restrictive way.

The NT understanding of the Temple

I noted earlier by way of comparison and contrast, the commissioning words of Cyrus and of Jesus. One was Jerusalem directed, the other 'all nations' focused. One gave a blessing of God's presence being with those who went to rebuild the Temple, the other the presence of Jesus (Emmanuel) with those who went to the nations. Given that Matthew is the Gospel that focuses on scriptural fulfilment, I think we can understand the commission to 'disciple all nations' as restoring the Creation mandate and the Israel calling. Those who follow Jesus will become stones in this universal temple.

It is not surprising then that the term 'royal priesthood' is applied to the church. In the context of 1 Peter, these words are written to the 'exiles in the Dispersion' (1:1), the ones who are scattered in an alien land. What better place to live and understand the true calling of corporate priesthood than scattered throughout the Empire? Peter reminds them of their 'royal priesthood' in the immediate context of Jesus being the stone the builders rejected. 'Chosen people' and temple language held together in the same passage. Likewise, in Revelation, it is to the church(es) located in the hostile context of Rome's dominion that John reminds them that they are a kingdom of priests (1:6; 5:10). Priesthood was not internal-focused but external.

What was the focus post-destruction of the Temple in 70CE?

Maybe some Jews kept a hope alive of the rebuilding of the Temple. This was probably why Bar Kochba in the (failed) second Jewish revolt of 132-135AD had coins minted with images of the Temple on it. If he was a true messiah, he could be expected to rebuild the Temple. But for the believers in Jesus, there does not seem to be a continuing hope for its rebuilding. And given the vision of Scripture and the belief that the new Covenant had been inaugurated, indeed that the New Creation had already begun, this is no surprise.

The vision of John of that final and total transformation with the descent of a cubic shaped city (which was also a bride so we must not think in literal terms) that had no Temple in it is breathtaking. No Temple, for the whole city is a holy of holies (the only other cube in Scripture), and the size he describes is of the then known world. The final vision is of no centralised building, no 'place' of worship, but of the awesome presence of God and the Lamb throughout all of creation.

We are those born of the Spirit and for whom all things are new, even a new Creation, and the challenge to live from the future, to have our lives symbolically and practically shaped by the future, not by the past is enormous.

In the following quote, I invite you to consider what church background the writer might come from:

> *The prohibition of Laodicea completes a critical cycle. The Lord's Supper had changed from evening meal to stylized ritual. The assembly had moved from dining room to sacred hall. Leadership had shifted from family members to special clergy. Now the original form of church was declared illegal.*

The writer was Vincent Branick, a Roman Catholic writer, expressing his convictions as he looked at the development of church from the Pauline letters to the fourth century (quoted from, The House Churches in the Writings of Paul, 1989, p. 134). Maybe surprising that a Roman Catholic writer would pen those words, but the quote shows how great the extent of the shift that took place over the first centuries.

I am not suggesting that the way forward is some iconoclastic movement, but I do suggest the church needs to rediscover the call to be an eschatological movement.

Pragmatism is a wonderful gift, but too often what was once developed to serve a vision, starts to dictate the vision and eventually its survival becomes the vision. That I consider is the highly insightful biblical perspective of the fallen city. The issue is not primarily over buildings - after all, we normally live in one of some form or another! - but of purpose. Sociologically I consider that the early church was a movement, one that was not primarily focused on its own survival, but on the transformation of the wider setting. This is the original call on Israel, and if she were to focus on that call, they would find that God would fulfil his promise to be their Provider and their Protector. Faith was necessary to live as a royal priesthood as only faith can sustain through the inevitable sacrifice required.

If I am correct in suggesting that Israel's trajectory was a fallen one and that Jesus has come to reverse that, we need to be sobered as to what extent we have embraced a, 'I saw no Temple in her' perspective.

We do need to ask the hard question concerning buildings, and our names for them. These things are important as even symbolism contains power. A tendency to refer to the 'sanctuary' is to apply temple language to a building, whereas it seems that the NT reserves such language for the people who are being built together for God's dwelling place.

Church growth programs... yes, they can all be agreed with under the pragmatic umbrella, but we should also celebrate (or even celebrate more?) when there are those who have been blown as exiles into a new setting.

Yes, there are many pragmatic tools that are so fruitful. In the suggestion that follows though there would be a challenge that could prolong the life of those tools as serving a godly purpose and not simply being served. How about once a year not simply thanking God for the tools, but addressing the tools directly? How about speaking to them and telling them that we will not serve their success, but that we command and commission them to serve the purposes of the kingdom of heaven. My experience is if we do not speak to the 'city' the city will speak to us. The city (institution/tool) is neutral but fallen so if they are not being continually redeemed, but remain unchallenged, they will revert to self-survival.

The body of Christ in all its settings is needed. But let us not sanctify it in one setting above another. The Temple is holy, and that Temple you are, said Paul.

Brief Excursus: A rebuilt Temple?

If we simply had the OT as our book, we might consider a rebuilt Temple as a future vision is yet to be fulfilled. The last chapters of Ezekiel can be pulled in that direction. Not so for the community by the Dead Sea (maybe Essenes?). They were already seeing themselves as the Temple restored, positioned due east of Jerusalem where the river was going to flow from the Temple. With all their quirks, they seemed to be a prophetic people anticipating a fulfilment more in line with how the NT interpreted those OT Scriptures than along some literalistic path. John in Revelation borrows very heavily from these chapters in Ezekiel, and he is free to interpret them in a non-literal way. As per the prophets of old and of today the visions are not normally fully understood by the original visionary. Maybe Ezekiel perceived a future day when there would be a glorious Temple in Jerusalem, but John borrowing the content of his chapters pushes us in a different direction all together.

Any restoration of a temple would be a step back; the re-instituting of sacrifices would not constitute a move forward. We live post-the-sacrifice, made once for all time and to end all sacrifices. We live seeking to align with the cornerstone that has been laid so that in that alignment of the new humanity there might be a living temple throughout the earth. Anything less than that would be a non-fulfilment, and not in line with the 'Israel calling'.

So, no, a rebuilt temple does not get my vote!!

A temple being built?

This is the process that I consider is still taking place. Paul writing about the one new humanity:

So he came and proclaimed peace to you who were far off and peace to those who were near; for through him both of us have access in one Spirit to the Father. So then you are no longer strangers and aliens, but you are citizens with the saints and also members of the household of God, built upon the foundation of the apostles and prophets, with Christ Jesus himself as the cornerstone. In him the whole structure is joined together and grows into a holy temple in the Lord; in whom you also are built together spiritually into a dwelling place for God.

– *(Ephes. 2:17-22)* –

And in 1 Corinthians again using temple-language he warns us not to be divisive, and in that context suggests that the alignment with a 'king' is a major issue.

So let no one boast about human leaders.
For all things are yours, whether Paul or Apollos
or Cephas or the world or life or death or the present
or the future - all belong to you, and you belong
to Christ, and Christ belongs to God.

– *(1 Cor. 3: 21-23)* –

The NT is clear that ministry gifts are important, but the ownership by ministry gifts of the body is forbidden. There probably still is the tendency within most of us to want a king, as a king will 'do things for us'. The trajectory in all its forms needs to be reversed so that there can be a corporate body that fulfils the priestly calling in relation to the nations.

There is a tendency to desire a king, and so we have to refuse all coronations and resist the temptation to search for a king. We have to take responsibility ourselves.

CHAPTER 7

SO, PAUL, WHAT WERE YOU DOING?

The previous chapters have sought to highlight Israel's bondage and fall from calling; they also underline that God's plan has not failed. That plan is to redeem the nations through a royal priesthood. The vision we read in the first testament and the Imperial context of Paul's world convinces me that he was indeed seeking to release a movement that carried a different message to that of the centre.

Adam and Eve might have started in a Garden, but their commission was 'the earth'. Jesus might have died in Jerusalem (and risen in a garden) but the commission was to 'go into all the world'. The *ekklesia* that Paul was committed to see in each setting was not a religious club interested solely in itself, but a representative of heaven's values who had imbibed a vision to see a whole world aligned differently. The *ekklesia* was a royal priesthood, a holy movement.

We might never know the content of the discussions that went on daily for two years in the hall of Tyrannus (Acts 19:9). I deeply suspect they were wide-ranging and were not simply daily explanations of a set of steps to salvation. Luke describes them as 'the word of the Lord' and the impact was incredible with signs and wonders. The message certainly made an immense spiritual impact, but it is also the city-wide riot that is of interest. The complaint was not simply that

Paul had disturbed the religious scene, but the economics of the city was under threat.

Paul wanted to respond to the riot by making a public appeal for peace, and not surprisingly, the disciples would not let him. They valued him and did not want to see him put his life at needless risk (Acts 19: 30).

It is, however, the next verse that carries the surprise. Luke flags the surprise with the opening word 'Even'. The disciples, and even some of the officials of the province, the Asiarchs, were committed to Paul's survival, with neither disciples nor Asiarchs wishing to contemplate his death. It seems clear that these 'Asiarchs' were not disciples... Here is the verse:

Even some of the officials of the province,
friends of Paul, sent him a message begging him
not to venture into the theatre.

What a powerful verse.

- Even, not disciples; rulers of Asia (Asiarchs being the Greek word).
- Influential people who were not disciples but were friends of Paul.
- These rulers of the land, who are not disciples, do not wish Paul to put his life at risk!

It seems that these Asiarchs were not simply acquainted with Paul but were some of his friends. Either they had not understood the personal aspect of being reconciled to God, or they had been unwilling to respond to the message, hence the word 'even'. And yet they valued this man and his message. Ironically the very message he carried was one that if taken seriously would either change the status quo or be so offensive that it would cause political riots. The

Asiarchs were the very ones (sanctioned by Rome) who benefitted by the system as was. Paul's message was hard-hitting and if acted on would have not only changed the social order but would have disadvantaged the very people who were his friends.

Almost unbelievable! I can only conclude that they saw in Paul's life and message that he carried a hope for the future concerning a new world, not a world to come in the sweet bye and bye, but one that was pressing in on the current order of things in the here and now.

It tells me they understood the (political) message Paul carried, the one he probably outlined many times in that lecture hall, had totally gripped them. In spite of the implications for them as part of the Roman order, they knew this was one message they could not afford to lose.

From the side of Jesus, a partner was birthed to pick up the mantle of royal priesthood, of existing for the sake of the nations. Paul believed this partner, not racially defined, but centred in Jesus, was to take on responsibility for the impacting of their 'territory'. Into locality after locality, he was committed to see an *ekklesia* develop that would be active in 'voting' for the future shape of that territory.

Many of those *ekklesias* were in a hostile setting; not many of them were impressive in numbers nor in connection, but Paul knew if they could grow in faith, then his work there was finished and he could press on beyond. To the church in Corinth he wrote:

> *We, however, will not boast beyond proper limits,*
> *but will confine our boasting to the sphere of service*
> *God himself has assigned to us, a sphere that also*
> *includes you. We are not going too far in our boasting,*
> *as would be the case if we had not come to you,*
> *for we did get as far as you with the gospel of Christ.*

Neither do we go beyond our limits
by boasting of work done by others.
Our hope is that, as your faith continues to grow,
our sphere of activity among you will greatly expand,
so that we can preach the gospel
in the regions beyond you.

– *(2 Cor. 10:13-16)* –

A major city; a city renowned for its decadence; a city with multiple gods and temples. And a small *ekklesia*.

The city was around 250,000; 'to act as a Corinthian' was a derogatory term used to describe unacceptable behaviour; meat sacrificed to idols was normal. And the church? Not the best example of those who had sorted out their issues! And given that Paul wrote to the Romans from Corinth, we understand that the whole community of believers could be hosted inside one house! (Rom. 16:23).

Paul so believed that the message of the crucified Jesus carried everything needed to transform the world; he knew great numbers were not necessary. Simply said, his hope was that the faith of the handful of Corinthian believers would increase!

In this booklet, I have tried to outline that the *ekklesia* was never intended to be a religious club, but a movement gripped by a vision of a different world, and therefore would plan (and pray, pray, pray!) and act in such a way that the world could be changed. The Gospel was not, and is not, simply a political message. At the heart of it is a faith that the central reality we all have to come to terms with is the death, resurrection and Ascension of Jesus. Neither though, is it simply a spiritual message that has private implications and one giving a hope beyond death. It is both spiritual and political; it gives hope and a practical vision for now because of what is to come.

The big vision of the Gospel is responded to by individuals. Those individuals are not often 'big' people; indeed, if one were to believe in election as God's sovereign choice of an individual,[1] we would have to decide God's preference is to choose small people! We might never be able to grasp the big vision that Paul communicated, but we need to understand that what we carry is for the world. In the next volume, we will look at the outworking, the small people whose small contributions are key to the future of the world.

1: I understand 'election' to be as simple as Jesus is the chosen one, and all who are in him are 'elect'; they have been elected in Jesus, who was eternally the chosen one: 'For he chose us in him before the creation of the world' (Ephes. 1:4).

New International Version (NIV)
Copyright © 1973, 1978, 1984, 2011 by Biblica.
The Message Bible (MSG)
Copyright © 2002 Eugene H. Peterson.
English Standard Version (ESV)
Copyright © 2001 by Crossway.

JOURNAL

- JOURNAL -

- JOURNAL -

- JOURNAL -

- JOURNAL -

- JOURNAL -

- JOURNAL -

- JOURNAL -

- JOURNAL -

- JOURNAL -

- JOURNAL -

- JOURNAL -

- JOURNAL -

- JOURNAL -

- JOURNAL -

- JOURNAL -

- JOURNAL -

- JOURNAL -

- JOURNAL -

- JOURNAL -

- JOURNAL -

- JOURNAL -

- JOURNAL -

- JOURNAL -